LIGHT IN THE CREVICE NEVER SEEN

Haunani-Kay Trask is known most for her role in leading her people on a path towards justice with her eloquent and sharply truthful voice, as well as for her unrelenting labors for what is right in a time of spiritual amnesia in the western world. Her poetry springs from this fight, which is born of a love for her native Hawai'i. — **Joy Harjo**

In her new book, the poems carry the emotional weight and power of twisted history and straight truth. The words themselves come from a stronger place in creation, one outside of a murdering history, and there is, after all, a nourishing sweetness here...rising out of destruction. — **Linda Hogan**

Although LIGHT IN THE CREVICE NEVER SEEN is, in the truest sense of the word, a book about Hawai'i, it presents a Hawai'i far different from the plasticized landscape envisioned by the tourists who flock in daily from East and West. — **Joseph Bruchac**

These poems are a deeply moving testimony to the power of a lifelong commitment to making a rich and graceful culture live and grow even in the most troubling times. — **Gail Tremblay**

Haunani-Kay Trask's poetry sings real stories from the heart of an Indigenous Nation trivialized through the tourist trade, as the infected blanket of the 50th state spreads over the bed of their Hawaiian homelands. — **Greg Young-Ing**

LIGHT IN THE CREVICE NEVER SEEN

LIGHT IN THE CREVICE NEVER SEEN

HAUNANI-KAY TRASK

CALYX BOOKS · CORVALLIS, OREGON

The publication of this book was supported with grants from the National Endowment for the Arts, the Lannan Foundation, and the Oregon Arts Commission.

© Copyright 1994 Haunani-Kay Trask

No part of this book may be reproduced in whole or in part without written permission of the publisher except in reviews or critical writing.

Cover photographs by Bob Weinberg. Author photo by Anne Landgraf.
Cover and book design by Cheryl McLean.

CALYX Books are distributed to the trade through **Consortium Book Sales and Distribution, Inc., St. Paul, MN 1-800-283-3572.**

CALYX Books are also available through major library distributors, jobbers, and most small press distributors including Airlift, Bookpeople, Inland Book Co., Pacific Pipeline, and Small Press Distribution. For personal orders or other information write: CALYX Books, PO Box B, Corvallis, OR 97339, (503) 753-9384, FAX (503) 753-0515.

The paper in this book meets the guidelines for permanence and durability of the Committee on Production Guidelines for Book Longevity of the Council on Library Resources and the minimum requirements of the American National Standard for the Permanence of Paper for Printed Library Materials Z38.48-1984.

Library of Congress Cataloging-in-Publication Data

Trask, Haunani-Kay,
    Light in the crevice never seen / Haunani-Kay Trask
        p.   cm.
    ISBN 0-934971-38-2 (alk.paper):$21.95. —ISBN 0-934971-37-4 (pbk.): $11.95
      1. Hawaiians—Poetry. 2. Hawaii—Poetry. I. Title.
    PS3570.R3374L53   1994
    811'.54—dc20   93-50813
                                                                                        CIP

Printed in the U.S.A.
9 8 7 6 5 4 3 2 1

ACKNOWLEDGEMENTS

Some of these poems have appeared in the following magazines: *Hawai'i Review; Bamboo Ridge; Chaminade Literary Review; Ramrod; Mālama, Land and Water; Ho'omānoa: An Anthology of Hawaiian Literature; Seaweeds and Constructions; Kaimana; Gatherings; Calaloo;* and *Chicago Review.*

The poems "Sisters" and "Woman" are anthologized in *The Colour of Resistance: A Collection of Writing by Aboriginal Women* (Sister Vision Press, 1994).

To the following poets, friends, and advisers, my *aloha* for their critical support: Joe Balaz, Richard Hamasaki, Kathryn Waddell Takara, Dana Naone Hall, the late Wayne Westlake, Joy Harjo, Joe Bruchac, Rayna Green, Eleanor Wilner, Gail Tremblay, and, most crucially, David Stannard.

And to Ben Webster, Errol Garner, Dexter Gordon, Coleman Hawkins, Oscar Peterson, and Keith Jarrett, for the music, and the love...

*for the blue-eyed devil
and all our years*

CONTENTS

Preface xv
Introduction xvii

CHANT OF LAMENTATION

A People Lost 3
Makua Kāne 4
Blood on the Land 8
In Our Time 9
Pax Americana: Hawai'i, 1848 11
Missionary Graveyard 13
Dark Time 17
Comin Home 19
Chant of Lamentation 23
Refusal 26
He'eia 30
Every Island a God 32
Hawai'i 33

RAW, SWIFT, AND DEADLY

Christianity 43
A Day at the Beach 45
Thirst 47
Kaulana Nā Pua 48
Woman 51
Nā Wāhine Noa 52
Kanaka Girl 54

Sons 55
Long-term Strategies 57
Sisters 58
Waikīkī 60
Love Between the Two of Us 62
Colonization 64
Racist White Woman 67

LIGHT IN THE CREVICE NEVER SEEN

Moon Over Mānana 71
Waimānalo Morning 72
Gold 73
Dawn 74
Koʻolau 75
So Tight Is My Love 76
You Will Be Undarkened 77
Menehune Night 78
Koʻolauloa 80
Ulu 82
Niu 83
When the Rain Comes 85
Haʻikū 86
I Go by the Moons 89

Pronunciation Key 92
Glossary 93

PREFACE

My people have lived in the Hawaiian Islands since the time of Papa—Earth Mother—and Wākea—Sky Father. Like many other native people, we believed that the cosmos was a unity of familial relations. Our culture depended on a careful relationship with the land, our ancestor, who nurtured us in body and spirit.

For over one hundred generations, we tended the earth. Then, in 1778, white people arrived on our shores. They brought syphilis and tuberculosis, iron and capitalism. And they also brought violence, the violence of first contact, the violence of plague and death, the violence of dispossession.

By the arrival of the first missionaries in Hawai'i in 1820, more than half the estimated one million Hawaiians present in 1778 were dead from foreign, epidemic diseases. Within another twenty years, the population had been halved again. Conversion to Christianity occurred in the chaos of physical and spiritual dismemberment.

In 1893, the American military invaded Hawai'i, overthrew our chiefly government, and put an all-white puppet government in its place. We were forcibly annexed to the United States in 1898. Hawai'i has been an occupied country ever since.

Haunani-Kay Trask

INTRODUCTION

Haunani-Kay Trask, the author of this first book of poems by a native Hawaiian to be published in North America, was stopped one day at an airport by a breathless American woman. "Oh," said the woman, "you look just like the postcard!" "No," said Haunani-Kay. "The postcard looks like me."

One of the barbaric absurdities of the Western notion that its seagoing men "discovered" places and peoples who were from time immemorial already there, is that such a discovery was tantamount to their disappearance. For shortly thereafter, the new arrivals began to make the original people disappear—both literally, through weapons and diseases against which the natives had no defenses; and culturally, by defaming and demonizing indigenous culture and gods and customs, by forbidding the language, by enforcing Western culture and religion in place of the native ones; and finally, by creating a fictional, postcard people out of Western desires—facsimile, cardboard Hawaiians to salve the conscience of America and sweeten the lure of tourism.

Exiled at home. The situation of the native Hawaiian—real people trying to live dispossessed in their ancestral islands; their language and traditions denigrated and forbidden by missionaries and colonial authorities; an impoverished minority where their chiefs once ruled; a people replaced in the public mind by cheap images made and sold in America; outnumbered by tourists thirty to one; their ancient lands, *taro* fields, sacred sites, and burial grounds covered with U.S. military bases, huge hotel complexes, golf courses—water itself channeled away to flush foreign tourists' toilets. It is these truths about the Hawaiian situation that few of us in North America know, but which are the historical ground on which the poetic figures of Haunani-Kay Trask move and find their meaning. To hear her over the noise of our own cultural background, it is necessary to turn to this context, to see Hawai'i through her eyes, and to know it for the first time.

Before you read her as a poet, it is perhaps helpful to know Haunani-Kay Trask in her role as a militant activist and public figure—a Professor at the University of Hawai'i, Director of the Hawaiian Studies Center, and a leader, with her sister Mililani Trask, of Ka Lāhui, a front-lines group in the current movement for Hawaiian sovereignty, fighting for control of the extensive native Homelands: "in every native/place a pair/of sisters/driven by the sound/of doves/the color of/morning/defending life/with the spear/ of memory." She is also the author of a book on feminist theory and the recently published collection of speeches and essays entitled *From A Native Daughter: Colonialism and Sovereignty in Hawai'i* (Common Courage Press, 1993), the best introduction to her political thought and public role.

Like all those who effectively challenge the status quo, she is controversial, and not just with the *haole* (the Hawaiian word for whites) and those of Japanese descent (the other dominant group in Hawai'i). Like Malcolm X, she has been demonized by a hostile press, and, also like him, the reactions within her own group have been mixed. Her assertion of a Hawaiian identity opposes the system of institutionalized and entrenched power and includes what Fanon and others called the de-colonization of native minds; it may, therefore, cause deep internal schism as ingrained alien habits of thought are challenged, as well as arousing fears of antagonizing the interests and individuals on whose power and support Hawaiian livelihood depends.

In all ways, Haunani-Kay Trask is a woman to contend with: like her volcanic islands, she is beautiful and gracious, but under that bounteous exterior is a magma chamber boiling with a molten outrage. She is a woman of *mana*, which, as she defines it, "is more than what the *haole* call charisma, or personal attraction. Leaders possess *mana*, they embody and display it. But the source of *mana* is not reducible to personal ability or spiritual and genealogical ancestry...it requires identification by the leader with the people..." (*From a Native Daughter*).

Ironically, because the Western power system has been closed to women, nationalist women leaders in Hawai'i are not offered the temptations of positions in the state political apparatus. And, says Haunani-Kay, "Caring for the nation is, in Hawaiian belief, an extension of caring for the family, the large family that includes both our lands and our people. Our mother is our land, Papahānaumoku—she who births the islands." Thus the movement for Hawaiian sovereignty—legal, spiritual, and cultural—draws much of its energy from the *mana* of women. And these women make it clear that whatever their affinities, their difference from *haole* feminists is precisely that for native women the concerns of the collective are the guiding impulse for the uses of power, and their collective is the Hawaiian people.

The poetry rises—delicate and volcanic, loving and furious by turns—out of this collective anger and anguish of a people, carrying the deeper feelings that her more public discourse armors with historical argument and oratory. Perhaps only a culture like ours, that isolates us by cloaking our commonality under a divisive and illusory individuality, could define art and politics in such a way as to make them seem mutually opposed, whereas they are, insofar as we live in a world with other people, inseparable. Haunani-Kay's is a poetry so particular in its lament for what is lost, in its litanies for the dead family members, for the desecrated land, in its outraged catalogue of crimes against life—that it is no stunted polemic, but a deep and accurately documented cry from the heart. As Toni Morrison has said: "It seems to me that the best art is political and you ought to make it unquestionably political and irrevocably beautiful at the same time."

In a spare and unsparing English, at times searing or razor-edged; at others, lyrical, tender, jewelled like the Hawaiian night, hers is a passionate and compressed poetry, a voice that is old in memory but contemporary in its combination of American with Hawaiian verbal and poetic means. The stark simplicity of the language, its restraint and exactitude, the constriction, the enormous pressure it is under, create the core power of this collection. If you read it slowly, as the truncated lines, large white spaces, and many short stanzas suggest that you must, if you let it work on you—the effect is hypnotic, and the accrual of power slow, imperceptible, like a reef being formed, word by word, until, like a diver in sun-struck water, you see the shape of the world that had been hidden from you.

The condensed, telegraphic style of these poems is related to the long silence that precedes her voice, as if it would be impossible to use many words, or to embellish a style, after so long a silence, so near an extinction. That silence and absence have become part of the very structure of these poems. Then, too, the sharply drawn, minimal images even of the most lush landscapes—

> slivers of sun
> pendulous rain
> ...
>
> I go by the *taro*
> velvet-leafed god
> flesh and mud...

—are an antidote to the tourist industry's parodic and hyperbolic images of a seductive, unspoiled paradise full of happy, welcoming natives.

With its open but compressed form and its spare diction, the lyricism seems wrung out of an English of which she is master. She has taken soul possession of a language which had once forcibly replaced her mother tongue, but which now she has made her own instrument, using it against those forces of domination to which language never finally belongs. For language is a living and fluid medium which is altered by what it takes in; in these poems Haunani-Kay has invaded English lines with native Hawaiian words that not only teach the reader key terms (with her copious notes and glossary to educate foreign readers and deepen the reading of the poems), but also take back the act of naming, setting native terms for things Hawaiian—the food, the land with its birds and flora, the sacred places, the gods. And these words also tune the music of the lines to the Hawaiian ear.

The English echoes the Hawaiian words; for example, her mother's home place, Hāna, and the word for family, 'ohana, set the rhymes and assonance in these lines: "...(by-pass Hāna?)/good thing mom's 'ohana/is mostly gone, only..." Or "I bring you/pa'akai, lū'au leaves/a bowl of sour poi/the wind blows cool/from Ko'olau," where, besides the eye-rhyme of "cool" and "Ko'ol...," there is the near rhyme of a "bowl of sour" and "Ko'olau." Haunani-Kay has described the Hawaiian language—which she was prevented from learning as a child but which now, thanks to a resurgent nativism, is being taught in many schools—as having the sound of water flowing over rocks. That music of melody and resistance, the liquid vowels with the percussive glottal stops and hard consonants to mark the stones in the stream, make a double statement in these poems: the Hawaiian words both affect the English sound system, and, in their scattered presence, their appearance as linguistic bits rather than full sentences, they remind us of the history that dismembered this culture and its tongue.

Yet they are the key words, and each word conjures up a world. As the notes suggest, these words are encoded symbols of loving and experienced relations to places, historical connections to ancestors, family relations with the land ('āina) itself. In "Ko'olauloa," its breathtakingly beautiful, pleated green plush mountains and waterfalls in the name itself, she writes: "this earth glows the color/ of my skin sunburnt/natives didn't fly/from far away/but sprouted whole through/velvet *taro* in the sweet mud/of this *'āina*/their ancient name/is kept my *piko*/safely sleeps/famous rains/flood down/ in tears/I know these hills/my lovers chant them/late at night/ owls swoop/to touch me:/*'aumākua*." In these few lines, she gives us the myth of the origin of the Hawaiian people from the parent *taro* plant, whose manner of putting out tubers suggests the proliferation of many from one, and the connectedness of the people to each other and the "sweet mud"; the *piko* is the navel cord which by custom the Hawaiians hide or bury in sacred places where they carve tiny circles in the swelling lava rock, so that the land itself is a body marked by navels, signifying the connection of this people to their land and the promise of longevity upon it.

And the *'aumakua*, she tells us, is a family god in animal form—here the *pueo*, owl—establishing yet another family relation with the natural world of Hawai'i. In these poems there is nothing like the traditional Western "landscape," nature seized and framed by the distant human eye. Here instead is a place inhabited by the speaker: "winter silk/under the palm," where the palm is inextricably both the tree and the speaker's hand, a world seen and felt simultaneously, without and within; where from the wounded earth "we hear all around us/seeping through the mud/a constant, inconsolable/grief," and where the land is so much a person, and the Hawaiian so intertwined with the land, that when she says "...rains/flood down/in tears/I know these hills/my lovers chant them," the ambiguity of the syntax and its freedom from punctuation makes it impossible to separate her tears from the rain, or those lovers from the hills themselves, the ancient chants from the sound of the trade winds in the leaves, the calling of the *pueo*.

The first two sections of the book move from the horrors of colonial history and the grief it engenders ("The Chant of Lamentation," Part I); through rage, in poems which draw blood from the smug, self-satisfied, and pious occupiers, and from those Hawaiians whom she sees as complicit in tourism's prostitution of native culture ("Raw, Swift and Deadly"). There are moments in these poems, as the section title warns, when the temptation is to turn away from what tears at us as *haole* readers, where our own sympathies turn against us, and we feel uneasy and even aggrieved at being in the target zone for our blue eyes or ancestral sins, or for the privileges to which our skin so wrongly entitles us. Well, we must feel what we must feel, for these divisions are in us all—Hawaiian and *haole* alike—caught in the cross-currents of a cruel history. But what is ultimately reconciling is to accept these torn feelings as the price of understanding and undoing that history, to put ourselves aside for a time, in order to listen to our Hawaiian sister. Like those on the island of Māui who go in the dark to see the sun rise at the peak of Haleakalā, it is with the assurance that what the dawn reveals at the heart of the volcano will be a beauty that required and requited the journey, and the pre-dawn cold.

The third and last section culminates the vision, permitting that inner view, as the poems turn to the extraordinary and wounded beauties of the islands, to the celebration and reclaiming of identity in concert with the ancestral powers of the place. In this section, the same slim lines that have characterized her poems throughout take on a somewhat different function, becoming a visible and verbal conduit or channel to carry and direct a rich flow of feeling, of living waters—rain, river, semen, foam, ocean—narrow channels through which renewal and illumination pour, as in "Light in the Crevice Never Seen." Like the powerful ancient *hula*, with its chants and fierce energies, the poems of Haunani-Kay Trask change our sense of the place Hawai'i, as her imagination allows us to share without intruding on this "drawing back/the undergrowth/to find temples/on the land." To borrow one of her titles: "You Will Be Undarkened." "Listen," she invites you, in her poem "Dawn":

>listen
>
>sea coming
>steadily in
>all around you
>
>*'ehu kai*
>on *kukui* leaves
>
>*iwa*
>in flight
>
>wind
>blowing
>
>the great red day
>straight at you

Eleanor Wilner

CHANT OF LAMENTATION

A PEOPLE LOST

like slaves from another
time, carelessly left
by a Christian
trader in some foreign land

strange unscented trees
from Asia and the Middle
East, great gouges of
Northern white

nothing familiar in
the Arctic wind   how
did this happen here?
my ill-clothed people
black hair freezing

in the American air
sores and frost on their tender
lungs, gasping for life
in our native Hawai'i

MAKUA KĀNE

I.

for a month I wake
to find you
in the stomach of
my sleep

shark's tooth
overhead
turtle guarding
out at sea

I bring you
paʻakai, lūʻau leaves
a bowl of sour *poi*

the wind blows cool
from Koʻolau

II.

in the shadowed light
I see you
young Hawaiian dancing
stories of the land

towards the bay
kānaka go together
to lay net

across the *puʻu*
giant suns
are showing off

aliʻi cloaks
of gold

III.

little doves
dart in and out

startled from
their banyan
by screeching cars

people throw cans
cigarette butts
plastic

in town, politicians
carve up land:
shoreline for hotels, valleys
for houses, underground for bunkers, sewers
miles of wire

IV.

our lives are made
now, all of us

brothers fish and plant
sisters practice law
and one of us followed
you, dancing

me, I fight
for the land   but
we feel there is
no hope

only sounds
diminishing
at dawn

V.

now, your daughter
wears your oldness
as a cloak

turtles disappear
at noon, a parching sun
scours the land

tonight, in the tomb
of sleep, I will bring
lū'au leaves and salt

we will wait
for the dark wind
from Ko'olau

then take our canoe to sea
with the dying
moon

NOTES FOR "MAKUA KĀNE"

Makua kāne—*father—is for my own father, dead since 1977. He, like his father and grandfather before him, lived in a white world which controlled our native land, Hawai'i. Both were long-time fighters for our people.*

The references to pa'akai—*sea salt—and* lū'au—*taro leaves—denote ritual substances at the time of death. For Hawaiians, the appearance of a canoe in dreams signifies impending death. And dream visitations by ancestors or others are considered portentous and in need of careful attention.*

BLOOD ON THE LAND

mourning floods the *'āina*
quiet oil of green
yellowing
lā'ī leaves

'awapuhi
crumbling at the root
lizard skeletons wildly
strewn

how the sun slits
the air   *niu* and *ulu*
dying against
pure mountain blue

a stronger light
from great seams of Ko'olau
not desperate
long and clear

falling with the flight
of *'iwa*

below   pesticidal
waterlands lazily
killing

sinister glare
off a smoking sea

and black
illuminations
as trees

IN OUR TIME

*In memory of Noa Tong Aluli
Hawaiian of the land, 1919-1980*

today, I went to the grave
no flowers, no tears, no words

the wind came up slightly
from the ocean
salt and warmth

you were the earth
as you are now

I cannot imagine
your life, being
younger by a generation:
all those children, all
that work, so much silence

in the end, your going
was familiar: a family
trial, burning nightly

certain to the bitter end
your sons, your wife
your daughter
myself

and now, there is
only earth, the salt
wind, a small
story of many years

I came to understand
but only the sea remains
constant and dark

    O Noa, we don't
    live like you anymore
    there is nothing
    certain in this world

except loss
for our people

and a silent grief,
grieving

PAX AMERICANA:
HAWAI'I, 1848

I am always falling
toward that dark, swollen
river filled with tongues
drunk and baptized

new priests waving foreign
flags and parchment
calling in the conquered
to hungry bankers

sacred places gone for coin
and rotting ships
diseased through
by poisoned seas

in greenish light
hooks and stripes
the lash across my face
and pale white stars

nailed to coffins
filled with dying
flesh cast off
from a dying land

only my scream in the homeless wind

and murdered voices

NOTES FOR
"PAX AMERICANA: HAWAI'I, 1848"

Seventy years after Capt. James Cook arrived in Hawai'i, American missionaries successfully pressured the ruling Hawaiian ali'i—chiefs—to divide the lands and establish private property land tenure. Our people had suffered a biological holocaust in the first decades of contact that reduced their numbers to a mere twenty percent of what they had been in 1778, estimated at over a million.

Stunned by the great dying of our people and believing that the missionaries' promise of everlasting life meant everlasting physical life of our nation, the chiefs converted to Christianity. Following the advice of the missionaries, they declared the Māhele, or Division of the Lands, in 1848. Within twenty years of this tragic action, nearly all our remaining people were dispossessed of their lands. The missionaries' children, meanwhile, had become plantation owners and sugar barons on the ancestral lands of the Hawaiian people.

Today the missionary companies, known collectively as the Big Five, still control much of Hawai'i's lands and politics.

MISSIONARY GRAVEYARD

for Bernard Trask, 1910-1976

I.

I'm *ono* for squid *lū'au*
and *poi*, fresh-made, grainy
...*mea'ai* for worn-out lives

your lonely meal
under a sunset dying
all our people
eating loneliness
together

II.

graveyard Hawai'i Nei:
coffin buildings, concrete parking
lots, maggot freeways

smell of death
smeared across the land

killing in the heart

III.

...a disease of the heart
out of breath at every street corner
going home with swollen legs
watery eyes, a slow burning
in the chest

there, by Pālama, you and your
father used to plant *taro*
the streams were full,
even *'ōpae*

down by Waikīkī
—it was Kālia, then—
old folks and kids
a meandering beach
no tourists

and up the road
taro and running water

IV.

our arteries have burst
darkening the beaches
immigrants scrambling
over us, and us
leaving for California

running from complicity:
the Democratic Party, Office
of Hawaiian Affairs

> your father tried: a little
> place for vegetables, some water
> but not enough for planting

reservation land
the *haole* calls it
no Hawaiian Homes here
just barren earth
blowing dust, dry
muliwai

and in Lili'u's house
a smiling Hawaiian
shaking hands with
money-men, eating
rice and drinking *sake*

V.

I hear that Hāna
is finally going: townhouses,
golf course, a by-pass
road (by-pass Hāna?)
good thing mom's *'ohana*
is mostly gone, only
their graves are Hawaiian

in the missionary graveyard

VI.

at 40, it's the hopelessness.

how did you live
till nearly 70?

NOTES FOR "MISSIONARY GRAVEYARD"

The line "no Hawaiian Homes here" refers to lands set aside by the federal American government in 1921 for the exclusive use of Hawaiians. Of the two hundred thousand acres available, less than sixty thousand acres are presently used by Hawaiians. The remainder is controlled by non-natives, including the U.S. military.

The lines "and in Lili'u's house/a smiling Hawaiian" refers to the current governor of the state of Hawai'i, John Waihe'e, who is the first elected governor of Hawaiian ancestry since statehood in 1959. Governors, including Mr. Waihe'e, live in the home of our last monarch, Queen Lili'uokalani, who was overthrown by American marines in 1893.

DARK TIME

a photograph: blonde edges
soft, afternoon light   reflections
of an unconscious time past

this morning, a pensive hour
hung with wetness   banana
leaves and sweet potato vines
blowing slowly in the marsh

the Kāneʻohe wind scented
with sad gardenia   torn
ulu branches   lost

Hawaiian men gathering
fern   sunk deep in mud
up to their waists   their anguished hearts
warm on the wetland

floor   broken Koʻolau ridges
immensely still   strips
of sun now   an egret flying
mournful cries of pigeons

a wash of light
misting upward
forming half an arc
of color: violet, red

green and gold   from
far away a familiar smell
of aging earth

coursing back through clouded
bloodlines to a young woman sitting
among *lauhala*   chanting

an ancient death chant
to the stars

COMIN HOME

for Kaʻohu Cooper
1959-1987

Hilo bay
was so *mālie*

aku boats
wen out smoothly

your ashes was
in da tackle box
wrap

wid *pua kenikeni*
your wife
an mom

throwin plenny
ginger from da farm
us guys had
Lily of da Valley

we was goin
sing but hahd
afta cry so much

back at da house
everybody ate
mosly coffee

at first, get
rid of da beer
from da wake

but den, *poke*
kālua pig an
cabbage, lots a

sweetbread, your mom
was strong, more
strong dan us

she tol
about your grandpa
how he came

in one dream
to your aunty
night befo

you lef, funny
da day was hot
afta all da col

kinda day
you woulda
bin at da farm

when *pau* fishin
all night, even
your mom said

you use to
go early befo
anybody got up

nobody had
chance
to talk story

little bit, play
music, neva
had time

to say
one *aloha*

befo you lef

why you wen
so early?

hahd for believe
you neva
comin back

NOTES FOR "COMIN HOME"

This poem is dedicated to my cousin who died shortly before his twenty-seventh birthday of a massive heart attack.

*The poem is written in pidgin, a local mixture of Hawaiian and English, because Ka'ohu and his friends spoke pidgin, which is mostly used by non-*haole*—non-white—people raised in Hawai'i. The use of pidgin by locals is often a political statement, especially in the presence of* haole. *Like Black English, pidgin has also come under attack as a substandard language that must be eradicated from everyday speech. Given the resistance of local people, however, pidgin is likely to remain the basic medium of local speech.*

CHANT OF LAMENTATION

I lament the abandoned
terraces, their shattered
waters, silent ears
of stone and light

> who comes trailing
> winds through
> *taro loʻi?*

I lament the wounded
skies, unnourished
desolate, fallen drunk
over the iron sea

> who chants
> the hollow *ipu*
> into the night?

I lament the black
and naked past, a million ghosts
laid out across the ocean floor

> who journeys from
> the rising to the setting
> of the sun?

I lament the flowers
aʻole pua, without
issue on the stained
and dying earth

who parts the trembling
legs, enters where
*the god enters, not
as a man but as a god?*

I lament my own
long, furious lamentation
flung down
into the bitter stomachs

into the blood-filled streams
into the far
and scattered graves

    who tells of those
    disinterred, their
    ground-up bones, their
    poisoned eyes?

NOTES FOR "CHANT OF LAMENTATION"

This poem is a lament for my ancestors, long dead, and for my land, scarred by American greed and cruelty. The ipu *is a gourd that accompanies chant and dance. The phrase "from the rising to the setting of the sun" is a reference to a traditional time period from ancient chants;* aʻole pua *means, literally, without flowers. The flower is a metaphor denoting child and thus, in genealogies (our form of history), a bloodline listed as* aʻole pua *is a line without children. The phrase "the god enters, not as a man but as a god" is a traditional reference to our great creation chant, the* Kumulipo, *in which life is born of the divine presence of both the human and the godly. The "disinterred" refer to my ancestors as they are seen by developers and archaeologists who continue to dig for ancient bones to clear areas for hotels. The "ground-up" reference is to osteological analysis which archaeologists perform—every chance they get—on native bones.*

REFUSAL

For K. W., class of '67
Kamehameha Schools

I.

I can't believe it
shot through the chest
in the doorway, pregnant
lover holding your little son's
hand, bags of dope
and beach towels
on the floor

didn't you think
not to open the door
killers waiting by two's and three's
in the death street below?

didn't you stop, dear one
just a second in time
holding sweet life
in your eager young hands
and wonder:

why our men beautiful
and strong on their running
feet, sun in their earth-dark eyes
why these lean, soft-lined men

go carelessly down
to nothingness
one after another, a whole nation
of men, Hawaiian brothers?

didn't you pause, my honey
on that threshold of death
glance back at your child
hesitate for life

before flinging it away?

II.

alone, here in the dark
with the women

fighting for the last
petal of blood
I don't understand

the eyes of our sons

so knowing at twelve
strange at fifteen
almost blank at
twenty-one

were you gone before
that, my brother?

down the white dusty path
to their carefully planned end
of your life?

III.

I can't believe
you are dead, my darling
the empty fury

of your death, the sound
all around me
bloody, silent

I can't believe
sons and lovers
shot, hanged, knifed
beaten, drowned

I can't believe
it will continue
like this
bodies of new life
flung down into death

I can't believe
a nation of men, a whole nation
of Hawaiian men, lean, handsome

and dead.

NOTES FOR "REFUSAL"

Hawaiian men between the ages of eighteen and twenty-four have the highest suicide rate in our islands.

This poem is dedicated to one of my classmates who attended an all-Hawaiian high school, the Kamehameha Schools, with me. His death, like that of so many of our young Hawaiian men, is not officially classified as a suicide. However, the number of Hawaiian deaths that are drug-related or occur as a result of "accidents" is much higher than that of the other major ethnic groups (white, Chinese, Japanese, Filipino) in Hawai'i.

HEʻEIA

I.

across the marsh
our lives flood
the grasses, thighs
in mud

a young rain comes
from lost Hanalei
that velvet-leafed rain
out of *taro* fields

we know
a lover's coolness
through banana trees

every half hour
jet booms
smash the air

but banana stalks
bend with the wind
compassionate

II.

a dream of return

sharp, green-tongued
pali

yellow-spined palms
laden with nuts

narrow ironwood
hills above broadbacked
rivers

two hands working
the mud
around dark green *hau*

thick
where the water runs

III.

the cleft ridge
falls away, silent

we don't see
the light weeping
great nets
of hair

tangled in death

the expiring day
already dead

we miss the stilt's
cry, a harsh sun
burning dust

into the night

we hear all around us
seeping through the mud

a constant, inconsolable
grief

long after moonrise

EVERY ISLAND A GOD

every island a god
wild with grasses of light
dishevelled rivers
bloodshot waterfalls

lost in the cities
in the foliage of herds
confused and red, beautiful
trembling clouds

going down with the night
of our deities

HAWAI'I

I.

The smell of the sea
at Hale'iwa, mixed with
early smoke, a fire
for fish and buttered clams

in a rapturous morning.
Vines of *naupaka*
leafy and stiff over

the puckered sand
and that ruddy face
coming from cold breakers

mesmerized by the sun.

They take our pleasures
thoughtlessly.

II.

The *kōlea* stilts its way
through drooping ironwoods
thickened by the fat
of our land. It will eat

ravenous, depart rich,
return magnificent
in blacks and golds.

Haole plover
plundering the archipelagoes
of our world.

And we, gorging ourselves
on lost shells
blowing a tourist conch

into the wounds
of catastrophe.

III.

The dancer's hem catches
a splintered stair. Descending
in a crash of couture

she winces over a broken
toe, hating the glittering
prison of Waikīkī

but smiling stiffly
into the haze of white faces;
a spiteful whiteness

in the reef-ringed island
world of her people

now hawking adverts
in their lilting pidgin;
filthy asphalt feet

unaccustomed to muddy
loʻi, kicking
Cadillac tires

for a living.

IV.

Green-toothed *moʻo* of Kauaʻi
raises his *moʻo* tail
peaked in fury.

A rasping tongue hisses
in rivulets to the burning sea.

Near the estuary mouth
heiau stones lie crushed
beneath purple resort

toilets: Civilization's
fecal vision

in the native
heart of darkness.

V.

Glint of life
in the graveyard's ghost
one yellowed eye

and a swell of heat:
two thousand bodies
exhumed for Japanese

money, developers' dreams,
and the archaeology
of *haole* knowledge.

Māui, our own fierce *akua*
disembowelled
by the golden shovel
of Empire.

VI.

*E Pele e, fire-eater
from Kahiki.*

Breath of Papa's life
miraculously becomes
Energy, stink with

sulfurous sores. Hiʻiaka
wilting in her wild home:
black *lehua*, shrivelled
pūkiawe, unborn *ʻaʻaliʻi*.

Far down her eastern flank
the gourd of Lono dries
broken on the temple wall.

Cracked lava stones
fresh with tears, sprout
thorny vines, thick
and foreign.

VII.

From the frozen heavens
a dense vapor
colored like the skin

of burnt milk, descending
onto our fields, and
mountains and waters

into the recesses
of our poisoned
naʻau.

VIII.

And what do we know
of them, these foreigners
these Americans?

Nothing. We know
nothing.

Except a foul stench
among our children

and a long hollow
of mourning
in our *maʻi*.

NOTES FOR "HAWAI'I"

Part II. The kōlea, *or Pacific golden plover, is a richly colored migratory bird that arrives in Hawai'i about August and departs for Alaska in May. Usually the* kōlea *arrives as a thin, almost emaciated stilt but leaves fattened and beautiful. According to Mary Kawena Pukui, the expression* haole kī kōlea *refers to the "plover-shooting white man" and was said "in astonishment and horror at the white man's shooting of the plovers, contrasting with the laborious Hawaiian methods of catching plovers, a way of saying that white people are strange and different." Today,* haole *who exploit Hawai'i, especially developers and tourists, are referred to as* kōlea *by many Hawaiians.*

Part IV. Along the Wailua River, Kaua'i, are found some of the oldest heiau, *or sacred temples, in the Hawaiian archipelago. One of these* heiau *rests on the sand at the estuary of the Wailua River. A large hotel complex has been built adjacent to it, with guest restrooms built on it.*

Part V. At Honokāhua, Māui, a large Hawaiian cemetery containing perhaps two thousand or more ancient Hawaiian skeletons was threatened with destruction, including disinterment of the burials, to make way for a Ritz-Carlton mega-resort. The cemetery was on land owned by a missionary-descendant whose hotel was to be funded by a silent Japanese investor. A huge outcry among Hawaiians stopped the disinterment and led the state of Hawai'i to purchase the land. While this episode ended well, the disinterment of Hawaiian burials for all manner of resort and residential development continues.

Part VI. Papa—Earth Mother—and Wākea—Sky Father—are progenitors of the Hawaiian people. Geothermal energy development on Hawai'i Island threatens the sanctity of Pele, Hawaiian deity of the volcano, and her sister, Hi'iaka, deity of the forest. Pele and her family were originally from Kahiki in the South Pacific and migrated to the Big Island of Hawai'i after a long and dangerous journey across the Hawaiian archipelago. Today, Pele and her family continue to be worshiped by practitioners of the Hawaiian religion and members of hula hālau, or dance academies.

Part VII. Na'au *means, literally, intestines. But metaphorically,* na'au *also represents what the heart means to Westerners, that is, the home of emotions, of understanding.* Na'au can also refer, in a figurative sense, to a child.

Part VIII. Our Hawaiian lāhui, *or nation, is now inundated by a foreign culture and people whose practices are antithetical to the Hawaiian cosmology in which the universe is a creation of familial relations. Therefore, all family members (the earth, the people) must be cared for and protected. The* ma'i, *or genitals, are honored by our people (as in* mele ma'i, *or genital chants) as the source of our continuity. Thus the "hollow/of mourning/in our* ma'i" *refers to our dying out as a nation, as a people.*

RAW, SWIFT, AND DEADLY

CHRISTIANITY

loves God's children
not the infidel
or African

but Europeans
Americans

Saints who came
bringing God's love

saw black and red
naked genitals
nothing so pale

as eternal
afterlife   white
civilization

spread over continents
blankets of disease
crusading armies

a slave's hand
cut off at the wrist
a desert tribe

driven into the snow
God's justice   white
death   white cold

cleansing the land
of blackness   sin
of color   every surviving

primitive   a Christian
reciting scripture
genuflecting on

broken knees
enduring penance
for dark skin   dark hearts

trying to find white
reflections
in the past   quarter-white

grandmother   pure
English   great-great
grandfather   blue

eyes in place
of black   vacant
as tombstones

children of God
brought out of
darkness   bearing

the mark of salvation

A DAY AT THE BEACH

I came to write about
the land   *'āina hānau*

but all the *haole*
drifted out
clotted on the beach
in tourist shirts
and white pants

barking dogs
above a roiling sea

I flinched
from the lack
of color   strange blots
against the purple
water

   in the distance
   mountains float
   dark and hot

   women carry
   baskets of shrimp
   upland to the moon

but here
the wind
is brittle
my images
constricted

by the snake
green eyes
of *haole*
women flicking
their tongues
at the scaly air

THIRST

for Kahoʻolawe

barrenness enters
a wooden lance
splitting sheathes
with the hardened
gleam of lust

we are parching
in the glare
our kernels grizzled
by a strutting sun

we are combustible

KAULANA NĀ PUA

I.

Morning rains wash
the damp sand cool
and grainy. Over
the cream of foam, young
surfers hover, tense
for the rising glory.

Beyond Ka'ena, a horned moon
drifts, green chatter-chatter
of coconut leaves
expectant in the mist.

Three dark children, strong
and gnarled, tussle
near the shore
little fists raised
in a mimic of power.

A passing tourist
florid in his prints
stoops for direction

when a sudden hiss of blade
slashed haphazardly upwards
finds his bluest
eye.

II.

Jets of red
splatter the fresh salt
of morning, one staggering figure
stunned into blindness
hearing stained voices
in the ocean's thunder.

III.

Running over old
rippled dunes, the children
sing-song a tune
out of time, time past

when their tribe
was a nation
and their nation, the great
lava mother, Hawai'i.

Not yet do they know, not yet
the bitter pity
of the past, even as they sing it:

Kaulana Nā Pua
"Famous Are the Children,"

taking the far curve
of the beach
in the bright glare
of day.

NOTES FOR "KAULANA NĀ PUA"

Kaulana Nā Pua *(literally, "famous are the children") refers to a protest song written by Ellen Wright Prendergast. The song urges Hawaiians to oppose the overthrow of the Hawaiian government by U.S. marines in 1893. Annexation to the United States is called an evil that will take from Hawaiians their beloved birthright. According to* Nā Mele ō Hawai'i Nei, *"The song was considered sacred and not for dancing. Four famous chiefs are mentioned as symbols of their lands: Keawe of Hawai'i, Pi'ilani of the bays with names beginning Hono on Māui, Mano of Kaua'i, and Kakuhihewa of O'ahu."*

Members of the Royal Hawaiian Band, on strike because of the overthrow, urged Mrs. Prendergast to compose the song because, they argued, "We will not follow this new government. We will not sign the haole's *paper, but will be satisfied with all that is left to us, the stones, the mystic food of our native land."*

This song is also called "Mele 'Ai Pōhaku" (Stone-Eating Song) and "Mele Aloha 'Āina" (Patriot's Song). It has become an anthem in the contemporary Hawaiian sovereignty movement.

WOMAN

Where are you drawn
to: moon, mountains
long, hard beaches
at starless midnight?

Or does the sound
of thunder incite
and frighten you
to come closer

over the shallows
into the arms
of those astride
a sun-burnt sea?

Sharks and mantas
under the surface
dangerous
against the blue.

Waiting for you:
your sullen blood
your silver eye
your fanged desire

to be raw
swift
and deadly.

NĀ WĀHINE NOA

Rise up, women gods.
Have Hina as your goddess
virgin, volcanic
unto herself.

Without masters, marriages
lying parasite men.
Unto her self:
a wise eroticism

moondrawn by the tides
culling love
from great gestating Pō
massive night

birthing women's dreams:
magma bodies
flowing volcanoes
toward moonred skies.

NOTES FOR "NĀ WĀHINE NOA"

The title means "free women" in the sense of those released from the restrictive Hawaiian system of kapu *(taboo) where, among other divisions and proscriptions, the genders were separated and women were considered defiling.*

Hina—goddess of the moon—is a woman who beats kapa— *bark cloth used for traditional clothing—in the night sky. She is a woman free of husbands and other men because she has escaped to the heavens.*

KANAKA GIRL

I.

Trying to find you
between Japanese
tourists and *haole*
honeymooners

dragging your skirts
and dying *lei*
like silent chains.
What's this song

of love about? A woman
who left her husband
for Oʻahu, only returning
when a *mele* unlocked

by seashells called
her home to Hāna.
Did you tell anyone
your name?

   Leilani and the Surfriders
   appearing nightly
   two shows, 9 and 11
   except Mondays

II.

Sounds like someone
nobody knows.

SONS

Your grandmother said
about your grandfather
"I gave him three sons."

Yesterday, a man told me
to give him trust.

Is trust like a son?
Or less, not being generative
phallic, or immortal.

Did she tell me about
her giving
in pride or warning?

But I have no sons
to give, no line of
immortality.

I am slyly
reproductive: ideas
books, history
politics, reproducing

the rope of resistance
for unborn generations.

But sons are not
so earthbound. They soar
beyond, somewhere

with a woman's trust
in their fists.

And I,
I stay behind
weaving fine baskets
of resilience

to carry our daughters in.

LONG-TERM STRATEGIES

We can't rape men
put anything in them
against their will

pull down their secrets
chilled by fear, or force

tight apertures
fresh and wide.

We can't stalk and take
bleed the night

squeeze hysteria
from burning stars.

No, we cannot do
just what men do.

But in Pele's hills
beneath a bloody moon
young women dancers

learn castration
as an art.

SISTERS

for Mililani

I.

doves in the rain

mornings above
Kāneʻohe bay   blue
sheen stillness
across long waters gliding
to Coconut Island

channels of sound
color   rhythmic
currents   shell
picking   jellyfish
hunting   squeals
of mischief oblivious
in the calm

II.

rain pours
steady   clouding
the light   dark
mornings   darker
evenings   silted
in the night   smell of dead
fish   dead
limu   dead
reef

eight million
for Coconut Island
five hundred thousand
for townhouses
on the hill   traffic
and greedy foreigners
by the mile

III.

destruction as a way
of life   clever
haole culture
killing as it goes

"no stone
left unturned"
no people
left untouched

IV.

in every native
place   a pair
of sisters
driven by the sound
of doves

the color of
morning

defending life
with the spear
of memory

WAIKĪKĪ

all those 5 gallon
toilets   flushing
away tourist waste
into our waters

Waikīkī   home
of *aliʻi*
sewer center
of Hawaiʻi

8 billion dollar
beach   secret
rendezvous for
pimps

Hong Kong hoodlums
Japanese capitalists
haole punkers

condo units
of disease
drug traffic
child porn

AIDS   herpes
old fashioned
syphilis
gangland murder

gifts of industrial
culture for primitive
island people
in need

of uplift   discipline
complexity   sense
of a larger world
beyond

their careful *taro*
gardens   chiefly
politics, lowly
gods

Waikīkī: exemplar
of Western ingenuity
standing guard against

the sex life
of savages

the onslaught of barbarians

LOVE BETWEEN THE TWO OF US

I.

because I thought the *haole*
never admit wrong
without bitterness
and guilt

without attacking us
for uncovering them

I didn't believe you

I thought you were star-crossed
a Shakespearean figure
of ridiculous posturing

you know, to be or not to be
the missionary rescue team
about to save
a foul, "primitive" soul

with murder
in its flesh

II.

we all know *haole* "love"
bounded by race
and power and the heavy
fist of lust

(missionaries came
to save
by taking)

how could I possibly believe?

why should any Hawaiian believe?

but it is a year
and I am stunned
by your humility
your sorrow for my people

your chosen separation
from that which is *haole*

I wonder at the resolve
in your clear blue eye

III.

do you understand
the nature of this war?

COLONIZATION

I.

Our own people
say, "Hawaiian
at heart." Makes
me sick to hear

how easily
genealogy flows
away. Two thousand
years of wise

creation bestowed
for a smile
on resident non
natives.

"Form of survival,"
this thoughtless inclusion.
Taking in
foreigners and friends.

Dismissing history
with a servant's
grin.

II.

Hawaiian at heart:

nothing said
about loss
violence, death
by hundreds of thousands.

Hawaiian at heart:

a whole people
accustomed
to prostitution
selling identity

for nickels
and dimes
in the whorehouses
of tourism.

III.

Hawaiian at heart:

why no "Japanese
at heart?"

How about
"*haole* at heart?"

Ruling classes
living off
natives

first
land

then
women

now
hearts

cut out
by our own
familiar hand.

NOTES FOR "COLONIZATION"

In contemporary Hawai'i, the phrase "Hawaiian at heart" is used by Hawaiians and non-Hawaiians alike to identify non-Hawaiians thought to believe and practice Hawaiian cultural values like aloha 'āina—*love of the land—and* aloha—*a familial love and caring.*

This phrase has been used by the mammoth tourist industry to lure visitors to Hawai'i and to congratulate those who return. The two groups who control Hawai'i's land and politics—the Japanese and the haole *(white)—consciously use "Hawaiian at heart" to describe their actions in the hopes of conveying some relationship to the land. In reality, the phrase is a cultural theft.*

RACIST WHITE WOMAN

I could kick
your face, puncture
both eyes.

You deserve this kind
of violence.

No more vicious
tongues, obscene
lies.

Just a knife
slitting your tight
little heart

for all my people
under your feet

for all those years
lived smug and wealthy

off our land
parasite arrogant.

A fist
in your painted
mouth, thick

with money
and piety

and a sworn
black promise

to shadow
your footsteps

until the hearse
of violence

comes home
to get you.

LIGHT IN THE CREVICE NEVER SEEN

MOON OVER MĀNANA

Water, golden water
gold on black
star water

from a distant island
glittering to shore
secluded dreams.

Our slow, meticulous
risings
a season of moons:

winter silk
under the palm
seductive spring

searing hot
crescents in summer
until this:

sly talisman
cast up from the deep
burnished and free.

WAIMĀNALO MORNING

deepens, erect
with purple
translucent reds

slow-eyed moon
drawing freshets
luminous

Koʻolau vulva
veined with heat
extravagant

light plunging
in long violet
shafts

penetrating
the carnal sea

with lightning

GOLD

is the color
billowing up
from *lauaʻe*   sweet
must green

dust, gnats, heat
at a slant

split
palm ends

sway of flaxen crust

storms of light
on the horizon
raining down sun

sudden steps
into the mango
showers
of glitter

something rich
and amber
settling
here

DAWN

for Pi'ikea

sit in
laua'e
long green gloss
between your thighs

split by sun

look up
at morning   flaring out nostrils
of night

love light
slung across
the eye
of Makapu'u

listen

sea coming
steadily in
all around you

'ehu kai
on *kukui* leaves

'iwa
in flight

wind
blowing

the great red day
straight at you

KO'OLAU

light in the crevice
never seen   mosses
palai   kāla'au
bamboo

crescent moon
stones
fragrant clack clack
from the shadows

hunehune rain
aloft on the wind
steamy rocks
falls of crustaceans

blue caves far
away   choked
with grasses wet
fully winged

high *'iwa* floating
many-chambered
heavens   still

and singing

SO TIGHT IS MY LOVE

so tight is my love
I come suddenly
into the deep of my heart

submerged minerals
rivers of night flowers
female foam hanging

from caverns of mud
you speak in gurgles
a great fish caught

circling the water
milky sperm dissolving
in spurts
of gelatine

hidden veins throbbing
with soft
down, pregnant

undersea moon
in a slender darkness
of brine smelling

of salt, the sexual
squid squirting his ink

to the stars

YOU WILL BE UNDARKENED

you will be undarkened
by me   led astray
to native waters
sunned until

old mango hills
rise leafless   you will come
long and flowing

poured slowly
through the gourd of laughter
spring of weightless

yearning   you will swell
at evening's light
rivers of you
flooded apart   and you will

beg me so
in your momentous showing
to keep you translucent
forever

MENEHUNE NIGHT

In the *menehune* night
below immortal stars
they come gliding

through *kukui* trees
silvery leaves behind

long spear of moonglint
on their path.

Near this wide wave
of sand, a cataract
of light, and all

the winds' little voices
laughing

out at sea. There
by new-born stones
a thousand children whispering

waʻa kea sliding
into surf, black
backed *ʻiwa*

tilting on the wind.
Far beyond, twinkling fires

streak south with
the shark:

*I Kahiki
Kēlā ʻāina i ka moaūli.*

NOTES FOR "MENEHUNE NIGHT"

The menehune—*mythical "little" people in Hawaiian lore—appear at night to help humans in all manner of projects such as fishpond building and wall construction. They are quite playful, often sing as they work, but disappear when discovered or disturbed by people.*

The phrase "new-born stones" refers to the Hawaiian belief that certain rounded stones near the shore reproduce "baby" stones. The waʻa kea—*white canoe—indicates the starboard hull of the canoe. And the phrase* I Kahiki/Kēlā ʻāina i ka moaūli *means "To Tahiti, that land in the dark blue ocean." Kahiki or Tahiti is the land over the horizon which Hawaiians identify as the place from whence they came and to which they return upon death.*

KOʻOLAULOA

    I ride those ridge backs
down each narrow
cliff   red hills
    and birdsong in my
head   gold dust
on my face   nothing

whispers but the trees
    mountains blue beyond
my sight   pools of
icy water at my feet

    this earth glows the color
of my skin   sunburnt
natives didn't fly

    from far away
but sprouted whole through
velvet *taro*   in the sweet mud

    of this *ʻāina*
their ancient name
is kept   my *piko*
safely sleeps

    famous rains
flood down
in tears

I know these hills
my lovers   chant them
    late at night

owls swoop
    to touch me:

    ʻaumākua

NOTES FOR "KO'OLAULOA"

Ko'olauloa—long Ko'olau—is the district on the windward side of the island of O'ahu that stretchs from Kāne'ohe to Lā'ie. The Ko'olau mountain range is characterized by razor-backed ridges, lush with vegetation, that display dozens of waterfalls after heavy rains. These mountains are the oldest in the Hawaiian islands, having deep valleys at their base, meandering rivers once teeming with fish and shellfish, and several wetlands in which our ancestors cultivated taro.

Throughout Polynesia, the piko—*navel cord—is buried or secreted away after birth because of its sacred connection to life. Where the* piko *is buried once determined part of the Hawaiian identification with home, or birthplace.*

The 'aumākua—*ancestral gods—are family gods in animal form that protect those who claim them.* 'Aumākua *are passed down through generations and require protection from their descendants. The Hawaiian owl—*pueo—*is considered by some members of my family to be an* 'aumakua *to us.*

ULU

come into manhood
testicles full
with seed   sweet milk
bubbling at the tip

great veined mass
hanging beautiful
to the ground   fed
by a dark groin of wet

hard leaves
oiled cool   and slick
fanned out in cover
from a leering sun

and below   the smell
of fallen fruit turned
sour   never having
been devoured by the gods

NIU

head in the earth
testicles in the air
in hiding?
or teasingly bare?

soft flesh food
dangling from above
clusters of *mana*
rather than love

sweet *niu*, lost man
perfectly made
flush my desire
by cunning display

NOTES FOR "*ULU*" AND "*NIU*"

In traditional Hawaiian culture, women were forbidden to eat ulu—*breadfruit—and* niu—*coconut—since they were male symbols and embodiments of male* mana *or power. One of our nineteenth century historians, David Malo, described the coconut tree as a man with his head in the ground and his testicles in the air.*

WHEN THE RAIN COMES

When the rain comes
put down your glass

leave the flowers
and go into the marsh.

Let her winds find
you and the great gray
clouds roll down around
you.

Let the smoke fill up
your eyes and the mist
wet your breasts

then fling off your
last piece of colored cloth

that she may see
and take you.

HA'IKŪ

for Lilikalā

I.

There is nothing
like this beauty

scarred by wires
from peak to valley floor

the whole expanse of rock blue color
volcanic wrath
fern and bamboo

disfigured
by *haole* power
burned through these mountains

with missionary lust.

II.

How long did those
ancients plant
in each sacred place?

How many terraces
constructed, fishponds tended?

What chants
commemorated
the goddess and her god?

III.

Millenia of love
rooted back into the earth
"vanished"

except for bands
of survivors, uncovering
loʻi, tracing genealogy

drawing back
the undergrowth

to find temples
on the land.

NOTES FOR "HA'IKŪ"

Since 1970, a cultural and political movement among Hawaiians has focused on protection and revitalization of Hawaiian language, religious and other historic sites, the practice of traditional taro farming, and finally, the assertion of self-determination as indigenous people.

Part of this movement was illustrated by a struggle to reroute a freeway scheduled for construction in Ha'ikū Valley on the windward side of O'ahu. One of the largest heiau— Hawaiian temples—*on the island rests in the path of the freeway. Students, workers, and Hawaiian religious leaders struggled in vain to change the path of the freeway.*

The poem is dedicated to Lilikalā Kame'eleihiwa, one of the Hawaiian women who led the struggle.

I GO BY THE MOONS

I go by the trail
of earth and green
slivers of sun
pendulous rain.

I go by the dream trees
flame trees hissing
and swaying.

I go by the shores
and coconut dunes, soft crab
sand in my heart.

I go by the temples
maile vines fresh
with tears.

I go by the *taro*
velvet-leafed god
flesh and mud.

I go by the thrust
of Kōnāhuanui
his lava jet
jewelled with fern.

I go by the moons
expectant
feeling in the throat
for the chanter.

PRONUNCIATION KEY FOR HAWAIIAN WORDS

CONSONANTS

p, k   as in English but with less aspiration

h,l,m,n   as in English

w   after *i* and *e* usually like *v*; after *u* and *o* usually like *w*; initially and after *a* like *v* or *w*

'   a glottal stop, similar to the sound between *oh's* in English *oh-oh*.

VOWELS

Unstressed

a like *a* in above

e like *e* in bet

i like *y* in city

o like *o* in sole

u like *oo* in moon

Stressed

ā like *a* in far

ē like *ay* in play

ī like *ee* in see

ō like *o* in sole

ū like *oo* in moon

Note: vowels marked with macrons are somewhat longer than other vowels.

STRESS OR ACCENT

Other than vowels with macrons, on the next-to-last syllable. Words containing five syllables without macrons are stressed on the first and fourth syllables.

GLOSSARY

'a'ali'i	native shrub with fruit clusters often made into wreaths
'āina	land, earth
'āina hānau	literally, the land of one's birth
aku	bonito, skipjack, tuna
akua	god, supernatural, divine
ali'i	chief
aloha	love, a greeting
aloha 'āina	love for the land, often translated as patriot
a'ole pua	literally, without flowers; flower is the metaphor for children; thus, in genealogy, this phrase denotes a line without issue
'aumakua	ancestor god (plural: 'aumākua)
'awapuhi	the flowering yellow ginger plant
E Pele e	E . . . e is a grammatical particle for a form of address
'ehu kai	sea spray, foam
Ha'ikū	valley on O'ahu, windward side
Hale'iwa	small community on the north shore of O'ahu; literally, house of frigate birds
Hāna	area sacred to the chiefs on east Māui
Hanalei	bay and valley on the north shore of Kaua'i
haole	originally all foreigners, now only white people
hau	a traditional lowland tree in Hawai'i
Hawai'i Nei	traditional way of referring to the entire archipelago
He'eia	valley and fishpond on O'ahu, windward side
heiau	place of worship; many kinds of heiau existed in traditional Hawai'i, including large, elaborate temples for human sacrifice
Hi'iaka	sister of Pele, goddess of the volcano
Hina	goddess, the moon
hula hālau	hula is the traditional dance of the Hawaiian people; hula hālau are dance academies that are currently enjoying a revival

hunehune	fine or delicate, as in fern, or mist
I Kahiki/Kēlā ʻāina i ka moaūli	"To Tahiti, that land in the dark blue ocean"
ipu	gourd, drum made from a gourd
ʻiwa	frigate or man-of-war bird
Kaʻena	northwesternmost point of Oʻahu, named for a brother or cousin of Pele; literally, the heat
Kahiki	Tahiti; also the place where Hawaiians return upon death
Kahoʻolawe	smallest of the eight major Hawaiian islands, used as a U.S. Navy bombing range from 1941-1992
kālaʻau	Hawaiian dance with long sticks
Kālia	an old name for part of Waikīkī
kālua	to bake in the ground; literally, the pit
kanaka	man, person; a generic name for Hawaiians (plural: *kānaka*)
Kāneʻohe	place on the windward side of Oʻahu island; literally, the bamboo of the god, Kāne; or alternately, bamboo husband
kapa	bark cloth used for traditional clothing
kapu	prohibition; sacredness; that which is consecrated
Kauaʻi	one of the eight major Hawaiian islands known for its lush beauty
Kaulana Nā Pua	"Famous Are the Children," a protest song written in opposition to the American overthrow of the Hawaiian government in 1893 and to forced annexation to the United States
kōlea	Pacific golden plover which migrates to Hawaiʻi at the end of summer and returns to Alaska in May; metaphorically, the term is used to describe people who come to Hawaiʻi to exploit our people and land, then leave fattened on our riches like the *kōlea* bird
Kōnāhuanui	peaks above Nuʻuanu Pali, Oʻahu; literally, his great testicles
Koʻolau	windward sides of the Hawaiian islands

Koʻolauloa	one of the districts of windward Oʻahu marked by deep valleys, steeply ridged mountains, and large fishponds
kukui	candlenut tree
Kumulipo	Hawaiian creation chant
lāhui	people, race, nation
lāʻī	*ti* leaf
Lāʻie	land section and bay on the windward side of Oʻahu
lauaʻe	a fragrant fern
lauhala	pandanus leaf
lehua	red, fuzzy flower of the *ʻōhiʻa* tree, a native hardwood that grows abundantly on the island of Hawaiʻi
lei	a wreath worn around the neck, usually of flowers, leaves, or shells
Leilani	woman's name; literally, the wreath of heaven
Liliʻu	affectionate name for Liliʻuokalani, the last chiefly leader of Hawaiʻi, overthrown by U.S. marines in 1893 and replaced by an all-*haole* planter oligarchy
limu	general name for all plants living under water, both fresh and salt
loʻi	irrigated terrace for *taro*
Lono	One of the four major Hawaiian gods, Lono represented fertility and was the god of the Makahiki season when all war was prohibited and feasting and games were held for four months.
lūʻau	*taro* leaves, a Hawaiian feast of good eating
Māhele	the privatization of Hawaiian lands in 1848
maʻi	genitals
maile	a native twining shrub with fragrant shiny leaves used for decoration and *lei*
Makapuʻu	rocky point that juts into the ocean at east Oʻahu; literally, bulging eye
makua kāne	father
mālie	calm
mana	divine power

Mānana	small island off the coast of Waimānalo, Oʻahu
Māui	the trickster god of Polynesia; also, the second largest Hawaiian island
meaʻai	food
mele	song
"Mele ʻAi Pōhaku"	"Stone-Eating Song"; another name for the protest song *"Kaulana Nā Pua,"* written to oppose the overthrow and forced annexation to the United States
"Mele Aloha ʻĀina"	"Patriot's Song"; another name for the protest song *"Kaulana Nā Pua,"* written to oppose the overthrow and forced annexation to the United States
menehune	legendary race of small people who worked at night building fishponds, etc.
moaūli	the dark blue sea
moʻo	lizard; reptile of any kind; water spirit
muliwai	river
Nā Mele ō Hawaiʻi Nei	*Songs of Hawaiʻi Nei*, a compilation of Hawaiian songs.
nā wāhine noa	the free women; literally women without *kapu*
naʻau	intestines; mind, heart, affections; of the heart or mind
naupaka	native species of shrub found near coasts and in the mountains
niu	the coconut palm, a male symbol
Oʻahu	the third largest of the Hawaiian islands
ʻohana	family
ono	tasty, delicious, hungry
ʻōpae	shrimp
paʻakai	sea salt
palai	native Hawaiian fern, important to Laka, goddess of the *hula*, i.e., of Hawaiian dance
Pālama	an area in Honolulu
pali	cliff or precipice
Papa	earth mother; originally, Papahānaumoku—she who births islands

pau	finished
Pele	goddess of the volcano; the volcano itself
piko	navel, umbilical cord
Pō	night or darkness; also the deity Pō, god of night
poi	the Hawaiian staff of life, made from *taro*
poke	cubed raw fish mixed with relish
pua kenikeni	fragrant orange flower
pueo	Hawaiian owl
pūkiawe	native shrub used for both medicinal and decorative purposes
puʻu	hill
squid lūʻau	delicious favorite dish of Hawaiians made with bite-sized pieces of squid in a thick juice of *lūʻau* leaves and coconut milk
taro	starchy tuber that is the staple of the Hawaiian diet; metaphorically, *taro* is the parent of the Hawaiian people
ti	a woody plant in the lily family found from tropical Asia east to Hawaiʻi
ulu	breadfruit tree and flower, a male symbol
waʻa kea	unpainted canoe set to sea after the *kapu* was lifted during the harvest festivals
Wākea	Sky Father who mated with Papahānaumoku—Earth Mother—to produce the Hawaiian Islands and, from them, the Hawaiian people
Waikīkī	place in Honolulu, world famous as a tourist destination; literally, spouting water
Waimānalo	land area and community known for its large Hawaiian population as well as its magnificent beaches

HAUNANI-KAY TRASK

Haunani-Kay Trask is descended of the Pi'ilani line of Māui and the Kahakumakaliua line of Kaua'i. She is a member of Ka Lāhui Hawai'i, a native Hawaiian initiative for self-government.

Her previous books include *Eros and Power: The Promise of Feminist Theory* (University of Pennsylvania Press, 1986) and *From a Native Daughter: Colonialism and Sovereignty in Hawai'i* (Common Courage Press, 1993). She co-produced the 1993 award-winning film, *Act of War: The Overthrow of the Hawaiian Nation*.

Trask graduated from the University of Wisconsin-Madison (Ph.D. 1981) and is the recipient of numerous awards, including grants from the American Council of Learned Societies and the Ford Foundation. She is Professor of Hawaiian Studies and Director of the Center for Hawaiian Studies at the University of Hawai'i. In 1993-1994, she was a Rockefeller Fellow at the University of Colorado at Boulder.

Selected Titles from Award-Winning CALYX Books

Natalie on the Street by Ann Nietzke. A day-by-day account of the author's relationship with Natalie (fictitious name), an elderly homeless woman who lived on the streets of Nietzke's central Los Angeles neighborhood. (Fall 1994)
ISBN 0-934971-41-2, $14.95, paper; ISBN 0-934971-42-0, $24.95, cloth.

Color Documentary by Lu Ann Keener. Poetry that exquisitely investigates our relationships with the natural world—animals and their plight in the modern world—while exploring the dominant role of humans and our own endangerment. (Fall 1994)
ISBN 0-934971-39-0, $11.95, paper; ISBN 0-934971-40-4, $21.95, cloth.

The Violet Shyness of Their Eyes: Notes from Nepal by Barbara J. Scot. A moving account of a western woman's transformative sojourn in Nepal as she reaches mid-life. PNBA Book Award.
ISBN 0-934971-35-8, $14.95, paper; ISBN 0-934971-36-6, $24.95, cloth.

Open Heart by Judith Mickel Sornberger. An elegant and genuine collection of poetry rooted in a woman's relationships with family, ancestors, and the world.
ISBN 0-934971-31-5, $9.95, paper; ISBN 0-934971-32-3, $19.95, cloth.

Raising the Tents by Frances Payne Adler. A personal and political volume of poetry, documenting a woman's discovery of her voice. Finalist, WESTAF Book Awards.
ISBN 0-934971-33-1, $9.95, paper; ISBN 0-934971-34-x, $19.95, cloth.

Killing Color by Charlotte Watson Sherman. These compelling, mythical short stories by a gifted storyteller delicately explore the African-American experience. Washington Governor's Award.
ISBN 0-934971-17-X, $9.95, paper; ISBN 0-934971-18-8, $19.95, cloth.

Mrs. Vargas and the Dead Naturalist by Kathleen Alcalá. Fourteen stories set in Mexico and the Southwestern U.S., written in the tradition of magical realism.
ISBN 0-934971-25-0, $9.95, paper; ISBN 0-934971-26-9, $19.95, cloth.

Black Candle by Chitra Divakaruni. Lyrical and honest poems that chronicle significant moments in the lives of South Asian women. Gerbode Award.
ISBN 0-934971-23-4, $9.95, paper; ISBN 0-934971-24-2, $19.95 cloth.

Ginseng and Other Tales from Manila by Marianne Villanueva. Poignant short stories set in the Philippines. Manila Critic's Circle National Literary Award Nominee.
ISBN 0-934971-19-6, $9.95, paper; ISBN 0-934971-20-X, $19.95, cloth.

Idleness Is the Root of All Love by Christa Reinig, translated by Ilze Mueller. These poems by the prize-winning German poet accompany two older lesbians through a year together in love and struggle.
ISBN 0-934971-21-8, $10, paper; ISBN 0-934971-22-6, $18.95, cloth.

The Forbidden Stitch: An Asian American Women's Anthology edited by Shirley Geok-lin Lim, et. al. The first Asian American women's anthology. American Book Award.
ISBN 0-934971-04-8, $16.95, paper; ISBN 0-934971-10-2, $32, cloth.

Women and Aging, An Anthology by Women edited by Jo Alexander, et. al. The only anthology that addresses ageism from a feminist perspective. A rich collection of older women's voices.
ISBN 0-934971-00-5, $15.95, paper; ISBN 0-934971-07-2, $28.95, cloth.

In China with Harpo and Karl by Sibyl James. Essays revealing a feminist poet's experiences while teaching in Shanghai, China.
ISBN 0-934971-15-3, $9.95, paper; ISBN 0-934971-16-1, $17.95, cloth.

Indian Singing in 20th Century America by Gail Tremblay. A brilliant work of hope by a Native American poet.
ISBN 0-934971-13-7, $9.95, paper; ISBN 0-934971-14-5, $19.95, cloth.

CALYX Books are available to the trade from Consortium and other major distributors and jobbers.

CALYX, A Journal of Art and Literature by Women

CALYX, A Journal of Art and Literature by Women, has showcased the work of over two thousand women artists and writers since 1976. Published in June and November; three issues per volume.

Single copy rate: $8.00. Subscription rate for individuals: $18/1 volume.

CALYX is committed to producing books of literary, social, and feminist integrity.

CALYX Books and Journal are available at your local bookstore or direct from:

CALYX, Inc., PO Box B, Corvallis, OR 97339

(Please include payment with your order. Add $1.50 postage for first book and $.75 for each additional book.)

CALYX, Inc., is a nonprofit organization with a 501(C)(3) status. All donations are tax deductible.

COLOPHON

The text of this book was set in Janson Text with titles in Lithos. Composition by ImPrint Services, Corvallis, Oregon.